FOOTBALL IN THE BIG TEN

rosen publishing's
rosen central®

New York

GABRIEL KAUFMAN

For my mother and father

Published in 2008 by The Rosen Publishing Group, Inc.
29 East 21st Street, New York, NY 10010

Copyright © 2008 by The Rosen Publishing Group, Inc.

First Edition

Library of Congress Cataloging-in-Publication Data

Kaufman, Gabriel.
Football in the Big Ten / Gabriel Kaufman. — 1st ed.
        p. cm. — (Inside college football)
Includes bibliographical references and index.
ISBN-13: 978-1-4042-1920-5 (library binding)
ISBN-10: 1-4042-1920-X (library binding)
1. Intercollegiate Conference of Faculty Representatives.
2. Football—Middle West. 3. College sports—Middle West. I. Title.
GV958.5.I55K38 2008
796.332'630973—dc22

                                                                    2007005409

Manufactured in the United States of America

On the cover: (*Top*) The University of Wisconsin Badgers on the field during a 2006 game. (*Bottom*) Antonio Smith and James Laurinaitis of the Ohio State Buckeyes sack Michigan Wolverine Chad Henne during the teams' November 2006 showdown.

CONTENTS

INTRODUCTION

Every fall Saturday during college football season, millions of fans pack themselves into crowded stadiums to cheer on their favorite schools. Ever since the first game took place between Rutgers University and Princeton University on November 6, 1869, fans have taken great pride in the accomplishments of their teams. Today, as success on the field translates into money and publicity, the stakes of college football have never been higher. Players practice and train year-round to be in peak condition for the season. Coaches battle both on and off the field as they attempt to recruit the best high school players.

The National Collegiate Athletic Association (NCAA) is the organization that oversees college athletics. The NCAA splits schools into three divisions based on each school's size. The largest

Game day at the University of Wisconsin's Camp Randall Stadium in Madison, Wisconsin. *Inset:* The Big Ten logo, with its "hidden" 11.

schools compete in Division I, the highest level of competition. The smallest schools compete in Division III. In football, Division I is split into two groups, I-A and I-AA. The biggest schools compete in Division 1-A. One hundred nineteen teams currently compete in Division 1-A football, and almost all of them play in one of the eleven conferences. Each conference is made up of schools that are located in the same region of the country. Teams within a conference compete against each other, and the team that ends the season with the best record is crowned conference champion.

The Big Ten Conference is the oldest conference in the country. Despite its name, the conference is now actually comprised of eleven large Midwestern universities. The Big Ten boasts a rich tradition—legendary coaches, record-setting players, and big games—and has a unique place in college football history.

The History of the Big Ten

The Big Ten Conference is the oldest collegiate athletic conference in America. Founded in 1896, just twenty-seven years after the first collegiate football game took place, the conference was created at a time when the popularity of college football was spreading quickly across the country. This was also a time when there was very little regulation of college athletics.

By Any Means Necessary

In the late 1800s, football was becoming increasingly important to schools and their fans, and teams began breaking rules to gain advantages. Instead of fielding teams made up of students, teams were paying professional athletes to play for them. Players were jumping from team to team, competing for multiple schools. When students were playing, the schools' academic standards were

A scene from the first college football game ever played between Harvard and Yale, on November 13, 1875.

ignored. Students who were failing in the classroom were allowed to compete on the field.

Football was also becoming an increasingly rough sport. During games, fights between teams would erupt. Students were getting seriously hurt while playing, since the protective equipment used at the time was not effective. Some players even died from their injuries. The situation was so bad that even the president of the United States, Theodore Roosevelt, took notice. He threatened to ban college football if the game was not made safer.

As problems continued to mount, it became clear that schools needed more control over their athletic teams. Purdue University

Purdue University president James H. Smart, pictured here in 1891, was one of the primary architects of the Big Ten conference.

president James H. Smart was one of the first people to take action. Smart was concerned that college sports were heading in the wrong direction, so he decided to arrange a meeting of neighboring schools to address his concern.

The Birth of the First Conference

On January 11, 1895, Smart and six other university presidents met at the Palmer House hotel in Chicago, Illinois. The universities represented were the University of Chicago, University of Illinois, University of Michigan, University of Minnesota, Northwestern University, Purdue University, and the University of Wisconsin. The presidents agreed that only full-time students could participate in college athletics. Students could not be paid to play, and players had to earn passing grades to be eligible to compete.

Using these rules as their foundation, the seven schools formed an organization called the Intercollegiate Conference of Faculty Representatives (ICFR). Members of the conference would compete against one another with the assurance that all teams were following a standard set of rules. After several other schools joined the league, the ICFR, which was also known as the Western Conference, would be called the Big Ten.

The foundation of the ICFR was instrumental to the development of college athletics. Shortly after its creation, new conferences began to form across the country, using the ICFR as their model. The National Collegiate Athletic Association (NCAA), which was formed in 1906 to oversee all college athletics, based many of its rules on the standards agreed upon at the Palmer House.

From Seven to Eleven

Many schools were eager to join the ICFR. Indiana University and the University of Iowa joined in 1899, and the conference became known as the Big Nine. The league dropped down to eight members in 1907, when Michigan left to protest a rule limiting teams to five games a year. Ohio State was admitted to the conference in 1912. When Michigan returned in 1917, the league consisted of ten members for the first time and became known as the Big Ten.

After enjoying initial success in the league, the University of Chicago had difficulty producing competitive teams in the late 1920s and 1930s. In an effort to maintain high academic standards and de-emphasize athletics, Chicago dropped its football program after the 1939 season. In 1946, it left the Big Ten altogether.

Chicago was replaced by Michigan State University in 1949. The Big Ten would then remain unchanged until 1990, when Penn State University brought its rich football tradition to the confer- ence. Although the league now consists of eleven members, the conference has decided to keep the name Big Ten for the sake of tradition and name recognition. The fact that there are eleven schools is represented in the "hidden" number eleven in the Big Ten Conference logo.

Rich Tradition

The Big Ten's famous stadiums, coaches, and players have created traditions that fuel the excitement of today's games. From innovative coaches who changed the way the sport is played to record-setting players and rivalry games, the Big Ten has had a great influence on the history and culture of college football.

The Big Ten is home to some of the best football programs in the nation. Its teams have won thirty-three national titles, the most of any conference. (In fact, Michigan has the most victories of any Division I-A school.) Big Ten teams also have played a

BIG STADIUMS, BIG FANS

It's not just the teams, players, and coaches that put the "Big" in Big Ten. It's also the stadiums and the fans that fill them. The Big Ten is home to three of the four largest college stadiums in the nation. Michigan Stadium, also known as "the Big House," is the largest and seats 107,501 people. Penn State's Beaver Stadium is the second largest, with a capacity of 107,282. Ohio State plays at Ohio Stadium, also known as "the Horseshoe." One of the oldest stadiums in the Big Ten, it currently seats 101,568, making it the fourth-largest stadium in the country. By comparison, the largest stadium in the National Football League (NFL), the Washington Redskins' FedEx Field, has a seating capacity of 91,665.

In 2006, the Big Ten had the second-highest attendance of any conference in the nation. In seventy-five home games, 5,449,439 fans passed through the gates for an average attendance of 72,659 per game. (Comparatively, the average attendance in the NFL in 2006 was 67,738.)

The Heisman Trophy is named after John W. Heisman (1869–1936), who both played and coached college football, and was one of the greatest innovators of the game. Above, the trophy is pictured before a game at Ohio Stadium, in 2006.

prominent role in postseason history. Michigan won the first-ever postseason bowl game, defeating Stanford University 49–0 in the 1902 Rose Bowl. Since then, Big Ten teams have made 226 bowl appearances.

In addition, the conference has a rich history of producing players who earn the nation's biggest honors. The Heisman Trophy is college football's most prestigious award and is given each year to the nation's best player, regardless of position. Chicago's Jay Berwanger won the first Heisman in 1935. Since then the conference has had fourteen additional winners, more than any other conference. The Butkus Award, presented each year to the top linebacker in the

CURRENT BIG TEN TEAMS AND THEIR ACCOMPLISHMENTS

SCHOOL	TEAM NAME	YEAR JOINED BIG TEN	CONFERENCE CHAMPIONSHIPS	# OF BOWL APPEARANCES	BOWL W-L RECORD
University of Illinois	Fighting Illini	1896	15	14	6–8
Indiana University	Hoosiers	1899	2	8	3–5
University of Iowa	Hawkeyes	1899	11	22	11–10–1
University of Michigan	Wolverines	1896	42	38	18–20
Michigan State University	Spartans	1949	6	17	7–10
University of Minnesota	Golden Gophers	1896	18	12	5–7
Northwestern University	Wildcats	1896	8	6	1–5
Ohio State University	Buckeyes	1912	31	38	18–20
Penn State University	Nittany Lions	1990	2	39	25–12–2
Purdue University	Boilermakers	1896	8	13	7–6
University of Wisconsin	Badgers	1896	11	18	10–8

country, is named after legendary University of Illinois linebacker Dick Butkus, who played from 1962–1964. Big Ten players have won the award seven times since it was first presented in 1985.

Conference of Champions

Michigan and Ohio State are historically the most successful programs in the Big Ten. The Wolverines' forty-two Big Ten titles are the most of any conference team, while the Buckeyes' thirty-one championships place them second of all time. Minnesota has won the conference title eighteen times; it's third on the all-time list. Illinois places fourth

MOST RECENT BOWL APPEARANCE	# OF PLAYERS TO WIN HEISMAN	1ST ROUND NFL DRAFT PICKS	# OF PLAYERS IN NFL HALL OF FAME	# OF PLAYERS/COACHES IN NCAA HALL OF FAME
2002 Sugar Bowl: LSU 47, Illinois 34	0	15	6	15
1993 Independence Bowl: Virginia Tech 45, Indiana 20	0	9	1	5
2006 Alamo Bowl: Texas 26, Iowa 24	1	16	2	13
2007 Rose Bowl: USC 32, Michigan 18	3	39	7	32
2003 Alamo Bowl: Nebraska 17, Michigan State 3	0	33	2	9
2006 Insight Bowl: Texas Tech 44, Minnesota 41	1	17	6	20
2005 Sun Bowl: UCLA 50, Northwestern 38	0	8	2	13
2007 BCS Championship Game: Florida 41, Ohio State 14	7	61	6	25
2007 Outback Bowl: Penn State 20, Tennessee 10	1	31	5	20
2006 Champs Sports Bowl: Maryland 24, Purdue 7	0	18	3	10
2007 Capital One Bowl: Wisconsin 17, Arkansas 14	2	22	3	8

all-time with fifteen titles; while Iowa and Wisconsin are currently tied for fifth, with eleven championships apiece.

Big Ten teams have won the national championship on thirty-three separate occasions. Michigan leads the way with eleven national titles, followed by Ohio State with seven, and Minnesota with six. Illinois and Michigan State have each won four national titles, while Iowa has won one. In all, six different Big Ten schools have been crowned national champion. (Penn State was not a conference member during their championship seasons.)

2 CHAPTER

The Coaches of the Big Ten

Big-name coaches have paced the sidelines of Big Ten games ever since the first conference game was played. From the University of Chicago's "Grand Old Man" Amos Alonzo Stagg to Penn State's legendary Joe Paterno, many of the conference's coaches have become symbols of the college game itself. These leaders are responsible not just for shaping the history of Big Ten football, but also for shaping the history of the entire sport.

Early Innovative Coaches

Amos Alonzo Stagg was a true football pioneer. As a player at Yale University, he was named to the first-ever collegiate All-America team in 1889. As a coach at the University of Chicago, Stagg contributed to football in ways that would forever change the game. Stagg's coaching career spanned seventy-one years, the longest in

Amos Alonzo Stagg, pictured here around 1932, led the University of Chicago Maroons to national prominence. He coached the university's football team from 1892 to 1932.

history. For his longevity and success on the field, Stagg was included in the first class ever elected to the College Football Hall of Fame in 1951 as both a coach and a player.

Under Stagg's leadership, the Chicago Maroons enjoyed an era of success that is unmatched in the school's history. From 1892 to 1932, Stagg led the Maroons to a record of 242 wins, 112 losses, and 27 ties. This record included five undefeated seasons, seven Big Ten championships, and a national championship in 1905. To honor their coach's many achievements, in 1913, the University of Chicago renamed its football stadium Stagg Field.

It is not just Stagg's winning record that makes him one of the greatest coaches of all time. It is also the many innovations he brought to the game. Stagg was responsible for changing football from a sport of brute strength to a more strategic game. Among his famous contributions to modern football are the center snap, the handoff, the lateral pass, the onside kick, the reverse, numbered jerseys, and the practice dummy. In addition, Stagg is credited with introducing such terms as "pigskin" and "cheerleader" to the football vocabulary. It's no wonder that, according to Hyman and White's *Big Ten Football*, legendary Notre Dame football coach Knute Rockne said, "All modern football comes from Stagg."

Just over 100 miles (161 kilometers) to the south of Stagg Field, University of Illinois coach Bob Zuppke and his Fighting Illini were winning games at a rate that hurled them to national prominence. From 1913 to 1941, Zuppke led the Illini to what has proven to be Illinois' most successful stretch on the field to date. Illinois compiled a record of 131–81–13 under Zuppke, including four undefeated seasons, seven Big Ten championships, and four national titles. He also produced some of the greatest football players of the era, including Red Grange, known as the Galloping Ghost. Zuppke, like

Bob Zuppke (*center*), pictured amidst members of one of his Illini teams, led the University of Illinois to seven Big Ten championships and four national titles during his coaching reign.

Stagg, was inducted into the College Football Hall of Fame's first class in 1951.

Zuppke was a blunt speaker, famous for his memorable quotes. It was his achievements on the field, however, that set him apart from his peers. His contributions to the game include the huddle and the screen pass, as well as the trick play known as the flea-flicker. Today, the playing field at Illinois' Memorial Stadium is named in honor of Zuppke.

As is the case with Zuppke and Stagg at their respective schools, the University of Minnesota's Bernie Bierman led the Golden Gophers during what was their best run of success on the gridiron. Bierman, who was captain of Minnesota's 1916 team as a player, coached the Gophers from 1932 to 1941. After serving in World War II, he returned to coach from 1945 to 1950. Minnesota compiled a record of 93–35–6 during his time on the sidelines, including seven conference titles, five undefeated seasons, and five national championships.

The Big Two: Woody and Bo

During the second half of the twentieth century, two schools dominated the Big Ten for the better part of three decades. From 1968 through 1982, the University of Michigan or Ohio State either won or shared the conference title every season. Since 1935, the Wolverines and Buckeyes have traditionally played each other every year in the final game of the season. For fifteen straight years, it was during these games in late autumn that the Big Ten championship was determined.

No two people personified this intense rivalry better than the teams' fiery coaches. Ohio State's Wayne Woodrow "Woody" Hayes and Michigan's Glenn Edward "Bo" Schembechler were both hot-tempered, no-nonsense leaders who despised losing. Each coach emphasized an offensive power running attack referred to as "three yards and a cloud of dust." Their similar philosophies can be traced back to the 1950s, when Schembechler played under coach Hayes at Miami University in Ohio. Several years later, Schembechler served as an assistant coach on one of Hayes's first Ohio State coaching staffs. This mentor-protégé relationship did nothing to soften their rivalry as head coaches in the Big Ten.

Woody Hayes coached Ohio State from 1951 to 1978, leading the Buckeyes to a record of 205–61–10. Hayes directed his teams to thirteen Big Ten championships, coached in eight Rose Bowl games,

University of Michigan coach Bo Schembechler shouts instructions to his players at the 1987 Rose Bowl in Pasadena, California.

and won five national championships. Most important to many die-hard Buckeye fans, Hayes had a career record of 16–11–1 against archrival Michigan. Hayes's remarkable coaching career was somewhat tarnished when he threw a punch at a player from an opposing team in 1978 and was fired. Nevertheless, Hayes was elected to the College Football Hall of Fame in 1983.

While Ohio State was enjoying great success under Hayes, Michigan was experiencing an impressive run of its own under Bo Schembechler. From 1968 to 1989, Schembechler led the Wolverines to a record of 194–48–5, winning thirteen Big Ten titles and making ten trips to the Rose Bowl. His teams finished in the national top ten on ten occasions. In his twenty-two years as coach, he produced thirty-nine All-America players. Schembechler's record against Ohio State was 11–9–1, including a 5–4–1 record against Woody Hayes. He joined Hayes in the College Football Hall of Fame in 1993.

New Coaches, New Champions

While both Michigan and Ohio State still contend for the Big Ten title nearly every season, the league has seen more balance in the past fifteen to twenty years. Several coaches have built strong programs from the ground up, while other coaches have continued winning traditions at their respective schools.

Barry Alvarez inherited one of the weakest football programs in the Big Ten when he accepted the University of Wisconsin head-coaching job in 1990. Alvarez quickly brought new life to the program, raising expectations and turning the Badgers into a Big Ten power. In just his fourth season, he led Wisconsin to the conference

The Lion King

Joe Paterno has been pacing the sidelines as Penn State's head coach since 1966. Since 1993, when Penn State played its first game as part of the Big Ten, the conference has been home to one of the most famous and accomplished coaches in all of sports. At the conclusion of the 2006 season, Paterno's 362–121–3 record gave him the second-most all-time wins of any coach in college football history. His forty-one consecutive years as head coach at a single school ties him with Amos Alonzo Stagg. Along the way, "Joe Pa" has led the Nittany Lions to five undefeated seasons, two Big Ten titles, two national championships, and twenty-one national top-ten finishes. Paterno has made more bowl appearances (thirty-three) and owns more bowl victories (twenty-two) than any other coach in history. His induction into the College Football Hall of Fame in 2007 will cement his place in the history of the game.

championship and a trip to the Rose Bowl. Since then, Wisconsin has become a perennial contender for the conference title. During Alvarez's sixteen years at the helm, his teams won three Big Ten championships, made eleven bowl appearances, and won three Rose Bowls. Alvarez retired in 2005. He is the school's all-time wins leader, with a record of 118–73–4.

Like Alvarez, current Purdue head coach Joe Tiller inherited a struggling program and turned it into a consistent winner. When Tiller was introduced as the Boilermakers' head coach prior to the 1997 season, Purdue had not played in a bowl game since 1984. Tiller's powerful passing offense provided immediate results, and the

Purdue head coach Joe Tiller celebrates a trip to the 2001 Rose Bowl with star quarterback Drew Brees.

Boilermakers earned a trip to the Alamo Bowl in his first season as coach. Through the 2006 season, Purdue has gone to nine bowl games in Tiller's ten seasons at the school, including a trip to the 2001 Rose Bowl.

Penn State's Joe Paterno was already a football icon before he coached his first Big Ten game in 1993. Having built one of the strongest independent football programs in the nation, Paterno was excited to bring his Nittany Lions into the prestigious conference. It didn't take long for Penn State to adjust to their new surroundings. In just their second year in the Big Ten, the Nittany Lions unleashed one of the most powerful offensive attacks in conference history.

Since 1966, Penn State's Joe Paterno has led the Nittany Lions to twenty-two bowl victories, more than any other coach in college football history.

They finished with a perfect 12–0 record, a Big Ten championship, and a Rose Bowl victory.

Current Michigan head coach Lloyd Carr has continued the Wolverines' proud football tradition by compiling a record of 95–29 in his eleven seasons at the helm. Carr is just the fifth coach in conference history to win five conference championships (he has won five titles to date), and his sixty-three Big Ten wins through the 2006 season are the most of any active coach. Carr directed the Wolverines to a perfect 12–0 record in 1997 and shared the national championship with fellow-unbeaten Nebraska.

3 CHAPTER

The Players of the Big Ten

Big Ten players have long shaped the history of the conference with their accomplishments on the field. With fifteen Heisman Trophy winners, seven Butkus Award winners, and hundreds of All-America selections, the Big Ten consistently features spectacular athletes whose record-breaking performances have a place in every fan's memory. In addition, many players go on to achieve fame in the NFL. Dick Butkus, for example, who starred as a linebacker at Illinois from 1962 to 1964, went on to a successful career with the Chicago Bears. (After he stopped playing football professionally, he found further fame as an actor.) More recently there's former Michigan quarterback Tom Brady, who has led the New England Patriots to three Super Bowl championships since 2001. Other former players have found fame far from the football field. Gerald Ford starred as center and linebacker for Michigan from 1932 to 1935. In 1974, he became the thirty-eighth president of the United States.

Long before he became a United States president, Gerald Ford was a star of the Big Ten. Pictured here in 1933, he played at the University of Michigan from 1932 to 1935.

Stars Who Started It All

No college player has captured the country's imagination quite like Harold "Red" Grange. A three-time All-American at Illinois from 1923 to 1925, Grange is widely credited with bringing football into the national spotlight. His enormous popularity was responsible for increasing radio sales (people wanted to listen to his games), the construction of large college stadiums (the smaller stadiums of the 1920s could not handle the crowds that he drew), and introducing the idea of professional football (people saw that money could be made from the sport). All of this can be traced to a single afternoon in

In a famous game against Michigan in 1924, Illinois' Harold "Red" Grange, holding the ball, runs toward the end zone.

1924, when Grange turned in one of the most spectacular perform-ances in college football history.

On October 18, 1924, Illinois played Michigan in a highly anticipated matchup. The two teams were tied for the conference championship, with undefeated records the previous season. Michigan entered the game with twenty-two straight victories. During that time, their defense had given up only four touchdowns. In addition, that afternoon the Illini were dedicating their new stadium to the men and women of Illinois who died in World War I. Emotions were running high among the nearly 70,000 fans who filled the stadium.

Michigan entered the game as a heavy favorite to win, but Grange had different plans. In the first twelve minutes of the game, he scored four touchdowns on runs of 95, 67, 56, and 44 yards. Exhausted, Grange sat out the rest of the first half. He returned in the second half, however, to score a fifth touchdown on a 13-yard run, then threw a pass for his sixth touchdown of the day. The performance was reported in newspaper headlines across the country, and the legend of "the Galloping Ghost" was born.

Other great players of the era included Minnesota fullback and defensive tackle Bronko Nagurski, Chicago halfback Jay Berwanger, and Iowa halfback Niles Kinnick. Minnesota lost just four games while Nagurski starred from 1927 to 1929. Today, the Bronko Nagurski Trophy is awarded each year to the best defensive college player in the nation. Chicago's Berwanger won the first Heisman Trophy in 1935, and Iowa's Kinnick was awarded the trophy four years later. Kinnick died in training during World War II. To honor their star player, Iowa renamed their football field Kinnick Stadium in 1972.

An Era of Excellence

The 1950s saw three Big Ten stars win the Heisman Trophy. Ohio State running back Vic Janowicz won the award in 1950; Wisconsin fullback Alan "the Horse" Ameche won in 1954; and another Buckeye, running back Howard "Hopalong" Cassady, won the honor in 1955.

In the 1960s, Illinois linebacker Dick Butkus was known for his ferocious tackling and was one of the most feared players to ever take the field. According to *Tales from the Chicago Bears Sidelines*, an opponent once noted that Butkus tried "to put you in the cemetery, not the hospital." Butkus won the Big Ten MVP Award in 1963,

THE PLAYERS OF THE BIG TEN

leading the Fighting Illini to the conference championship and a trip to the Rose Bowl. Today, the Butkus Award, established in 1985, is given annually to the nation's top collegiate linebacker.

The 1970s introduced one of the conference's most successful running backs ever to play the game. Ohio State's Archie Griffin, who was a member of four championship teams from 1972 to 1975, holds a NCAA record with thirty-one straight games in which he rushed for more than 100 yards. He is the only player who has ever won the Heisman Trophy twice, receiving the honor in both 1974 and 1975. Griffin finished his record-setting collegiate career with 5,589 rushing yards, which places him second all-time in conference history.

The 1980s saw the end of Michigan and Ohio State's reign at the top of the conference, and the emergence of star players across

THE TRIBUNE SILVER FOOTBALL AWARD

The Tribune Silver Football Award is presented each year to the Big Ten Conference's best player. Each school nominates its team's MVP for consideration. The winner is then determined by a vote of the conference coaches. The Big Ten also awards separate individual honors each season, such as offensive and defensive players of the year, as voted by the coaches and media.

The first Silver Football was awarded in 1924 to Illinois' Harold "Red" Grange. Since then, Michigan and Ohio State each have had fifteen Silver Football winners, the most in the conference. Iowa has had the third most winners with nine, while Wisconsin and Indiana boast the fourth most in the conference with seven winners apiece.

Recent recipients of the award include Purdue quarterback Drew Brees (2000), Indiana quarterback Antwaan Randle-El (2001), Iowa quarterback Brad Banks (2002), Michigan running back Chris Perry (2003), Michigan wide receiver Braylon Edwards (2004), Penn State quarterback Michael Robinson (2005), and Ohio State quarterback Troy Smith (2006).

Ohio State's Archie Griffin, rushing for yards in a 1974 game against Illinois. He is the only player in college football history to win the Heisman Trophy twice.

the league. Iowa quarterback Chuck Long passed the Hawkeyes to national prominence in the early 1980s. Illinois wide receiver David Williams broke receiving records at Illinois while leading the team to the 1984 Rose Bowl. In the late 1980s, running back Anthony Thompson ran his way into the record books at Indiana. Meanwhile, in 1989, Michigan State linebacker Percy Snow became the first player to win both the Butkus and Lombardi Awards. (The Lombardi Award honors the nation's best lineman.)

Continuing the Tradition

The 1990s brought more national honors to the conference's top offensive and defensive players. Once again, it was Michigan and Ohio State leading the charge.

The decade began with Michigan wide receiver Desmond Howard winning the 1991 Heisman Trophy. Howard's performance against archrival Ohio State eliminated any doubt as to who would win the award that year. Howard, a talented kick returner, fielded a punt on the 7-yard-line and raced 93 yards for the touchdown. Once in the end zone, he struck a Heisman pose, imitating the player on the trophy. Michigan went on to win the game, and Howard's Heisman pose is now one of the most popular and recognizable images in college football.

In 1992, fellow Wolverine Erick Anderson won the Butkus Award. In 1997, another Michigan player, Charles Woodson, became the first defensive player ever to win the Heisman Trophy. Woodson's out-standing play both as defensive back and kick returner helped lead Michigan to the 1997 national championship.

The 1995 season witnessed one of the most amazing turnarounds in conference history. At the start of the season, Northwestern,

Michigan's Desmond Howard strikes a Heisman pose (*left*) after returning a punt 93 yards against Ohio State in 1991. Howard went on to win the trophy (*right*) at the end of the season.

long one of the weakest teams in the conference (and the nation) was expected to finish in last place. However, led by quarterback Steve Schnur, running back Darnell Autry, and linebacker Pat Fitzgerald, the Wildcats shocked the nation by charging to an 8–0 conference record and earning a trip to the Rose Bowl. Although Northwestern lost, it was their first bowl appearance in forty-seven years. Their magical season will always have a special place in conference history.

Meanwhile, Ohio State running back Eddie George ran to the Heisman Trophy in 1995 after rushing for 1,927 yards and 24 touchdowns. George overcame early struggles with fumbling and finished

Big Ten Award Winners

The following list highlights some of the Big Ten players who have won national awards. While there are many honors awarded to college football players each year, the ones mentioned here are a few of the most prestigious. Many of these players have gone on to successful careers in professional football.

Heisman Award: Nation's Best Player

Year	Player	School
1935	Jay Berwanger (RB)	Chicago
1939	Nile Kinnick (RB)	Iowa
1940	Tom Harmon (RB)	Michigan
1941	Bruce Smith (RB)	Minnesota
1944	Les Horvath (QB)	Ohio State
1950	Vic Janowicz (RB)	Ohio State
1954	Alan Ameche (FB)	Wisconsin
1955	Howard Cassady (RB)	Ohio State
1974	Archie Griffin (RB)	Ohio State
1975	Archie Griffin (RB)	Ohio State
1991	Desmond Howard (WR)	Michigan
1995	Eddie George (RB)	Ohio State
1997	Charles Woodson (CB)	Michigan
1999	Ron Dayne (RB)	Wisconsin
2006	Troy Smith (QB)	Ohio State

Butkus Award: Nation's Top Linebacker

Year	Player	School
1989	Percy Snow	Michigan State
1991	Erick Anderson	Michigan
1994	Dana Howard	Illinois
1995	Kevin Hardy	Illinois
1997	Andy Katzenmoyer	Ohio State
1999	LaVar Arrington	Penn State
2005	Paul Posluszny	Penn State

Bronko Nagurski Award: Nation's Best Defensive Player

Year	Player	School
1995	Pat Fitzgerald (LB)	Northwestern
1996	Pat Fitzgerald(LB)	Northwestern
1997	Charles Woodson (CB)	Michigan
2006	James Laurinaitis (LB)	Ohio State

Lombardi Award: Nation's Best Lineman (Offensive or Defensive)

Year	Player	School
1970	Jim Stillwagon (DT)	Ohio State
1973	John Hicks (OT)	Ohio State
1987	Chris Spielman (DT)	Ohio State
1989	Percy Snow (LB)	Michigan State
1995	Orlando Pace (OT)	Ohio State
1996	Orlando Pace (OT)	Ohio State
2006	LaMarr Woodley (DE, LB)	Michigan

his Buckeye career with 3,768 rushing yards (second only to Archie Griffin in Ohio State history). Two years later, Ohio State linebacker Andy "the Big Kat" Katzenmoyer became the first Buckeye to win the Butkus Award.

Three other Big Ten players won the Butkus Award in the 1990s. Illinois' Dana Howard won the award in 1994, and teammate Kevin Hardy won in 1995. Penn State's LaVar Arrington, famous for a play known as "the LaVar Leap" in which he jumped over the offensive line to tackle an opponent in the backfield, won the award in 1999.

Wisconsin running back Ron Dayne won the Heisman Trophy in 1999. A monster in the backfield weighing more than 260 pounds, "the Great Dayne" used a unique blend of speed and strength to power himself into the record books. He currently holds both the NCAA and Big Ten career rushing records with 6,397 yards. Other recent award winners include Penn State linebacker Paul Posluszny, who strengthened his school's reputation as "Linebacker U" by winning the Butkus Award in 2005. Ohio State quarterback Troy Smith won the 2006 Heisman Trophy while leading the Buckeyes to the national championship game.

4 CHAPTER

The Games of the Big Ten

From traditional conference rivalries to the post season bowls, big games are the highlight of a Big Ten season. The memorable games are filled with great performances, thrilling victories, and crushing defeats. Every year a new chapter is written in the history of each rivalry and bowl game.

Conference Games

Many conference matchups are "trophy games" in which the participants compete annually for the right to take home a trophy. Other rivalries don't feature a trophy but are played for school pride and bragging rights over the opponent. Either way, all conference games are intense rivalries that have developed over many years. Since conference teams play each other almost every year, teams don't have to wait very long to try to reclaim bragging rights.

The Ohio State Buckeyes pose for a team picture in 1897, the same year their rivalry with the University of Michigan began.

Michigan vs. Ohio State

There is no better rivalry in the nation than Michigan vs. Ohio State. In 1999, the sports network ESPN named Michigan-Ohio State the number-one greatest sports rivalry of the twentieth century. In 2003, the U.S. House of Representatives passed a resolution recognizing the Michigan-Ohio State rivalry as the best sports rivalry in history. According to About.com, the matchup is so important to each school's fans that former Ohio State coach John Cooper once observed, "You can have a good season if you win the rest of your games . . . but you can't have a great season unless you beat Michigan."

The first game between Michigan and Ohio State was played in 1897, with the Wolverines defeating the Buckeyes 34–0. Since 1935, the one annual game between the conference rivals has been played on the final weekend of the season. On forty-two occasions this battle between conference powers has had a direct impact on the conference championship. With so much at stake every time the two teams face off, many fans refer to the matchup as simply "the Game." While each school has had its ups and downs during the course of the rivalry, Michigan holds the all-time lead with a 57–40–6 record.

The 2006 Michigan-Ohio State matchup was one of the most-anticipated games in the history of the rivalry. Each team carried perfect 11–0 records into the game, with the Buckeyes ranked first in the country and the Wolverines ranked number two. The winner of the game was guaranteed a place in the BCS (Bowl Championship Series) national championship game. The game took on added significance when legendary former Michigan coach Bo Schembechler, a central figure in the heated rivalry for years, passed away one day before the game. With emotions on both sides running high, Ohio State pulled out the victory in a 42–39 thriller. Buckeye quarterback Troy Smith (who went on to win the 2006 Heisman Trophy) threw for four touchdowns and 316 yards.

The Little Brown Jug

In the nation's oldest intercollegiate trophy game, Michigan and Minnesota battle every year for the Little Brown Jug trophy. The trophy's roots go back to 1903, when the Golden Gophers tied the Wolverines 6–6 to end Michigan's twenty-eight-game winning streak. In the chaos of the celebration that followed, Michigan accidentally left a water jug behind on the field. When Michigan coach Fielding Yost wrote a letter requesting that Minnesota return the

Michigan linebacker Shantee Orr holds up the Little Brown Jug after Michigan defeated Minnesota on November 10, 2001.

jug, the Gophers wrote back, "If you want it, you'll have to win it." This started the tradition of the winning team keeping the jug until they are defeated.

The score of every game between the schools is painted on the side of the trophy. Michigan has dominated the series by compiling an all-time record of 64–22–3. In 2005, Minnesota ended a nineteen-year drought by defeating the Wolverines for the first time since 1986. They soon returned the jug to Michigan, however, following a 28–14 Wolverine victory in 2006.

The Old Oaken Bucket

In-state rivals Indiana University and Purdue battle each season for the right to take home the trophy known as the Old Oaken Bucket. The tradition began in 1925 when alumni groups from the rival schools met and decided to present a trophy to the winning team. According to the Purdue Intercollegiate Athletics Web site, a representative from each school decided that "an old oaken bucket would be a most typical trophy from this state and should be taken from a well somewhere in Indiana." An acceptable bucket was eventually found in a well on a southern Indiana farm.

The bucket tracks the history of the games with a metal chain that is attached to the trophy. If the Hoosiers win, a link with a letter I is added to the chain. If the Boilermakers win, a link with the letter P is attached to the chain. Purdue boasts a 54–25–3 record through 2006.

Paul Bunyan's Axe

In 1890, Minnesota defeated Wisconsin 63–0 in the first meeting between the two schools. Since then, Minnesota and Wisconsin have battled on the gridiron 115 times, making it the oldest rivalry in all of college football. The game has always been intense, and in 1930 the Slab of Bacon trophy was created to honor the winner. (The trophy was called this because the winning team would "bring home the bacon.") The schools hoped that the trophy—(which was a bacon slab made of black walnut, with a football carved on its top)—would become as well known as the more famous Little Brown Jug trophy. The Slab of Bacon was stolen from the field following a game in the early 1940s. A new trophy, named Paul Bunyan's Axe after the mythical giant lumberjack, took its place in 1948.

The score of every game ever played between the two teams is recorded on the axe's 6-foot handle. Both sides of the handle have been filled, and school officials are now entering the score on the narrow sides of the axe's handle. Wisconsin holds a 32–24–3 lead in the series since the introduction of the Paul Bunyan trophy.

Bowl Games

In 1902, Michigan defeated Stanford in the first bowl game ever played. Since then, the Big Ten has been a fixture in college football's postseason. Bowl games have long been the measure of a

Paul Bunyan's Axe is awarded each year to the winner of the Minnesota-Wisconsin game. Here, the axe, more than 6 feet tall, is on display at the University of Wisconsin after the Badgers' 2004 victory.

season's success, and Big Ten teams regularly compete in the nation's most prestigious bowls. Conference teams have made 226 bowl appearances, which is especially impressive considering that until the 1975 season, the Big Ten allowed only one of its teams to compete in the postseason per year.

The current Big Ten schedule sends its members to specific bowl games based on their conference standings. In order to be eligible to play in bowl games, a team must have six victories over other NCAA Division I-A teams during the season. The conference champion earns a trip to the Rose Bowl to play the champion from the Pacific Ten (Pac-10) Conference. The conference runner-up takes on the runner-up from the Southeastern Conference (SEC) in the Capital One Bowl. The Big Ten's third-place finisher takes on the third-place team from the SEC in the Outback Bowl. The Big Ten also has made arrangements that send the league's fourth-through-seventh-place teams to other bowl games, though this is a relatively new tradition.

Since 1998, the Bowl Championship Series (BCS) system has altered the postseason landscape and changed traditional bowl pairings. If the Big Ten champion finishes either first or second in the BCS standings, they will play in the BCS championship game instead of the Rose Bowl game. In this scenario, the Big Ten's second-place finisher would play in the Rose Bowl game. If two of the conference's teams earn spots in the BCS game, the Capital One Bowl would select the Big Ten's third-place team, the Outback Bowl would invite the fourth place team, and so on.

The Rose Bowl

Nicknamed "the Granddaddy of Them All," the Rose Bowl has long been a highlight of the bowl season. Every year, it features two of the highest-ranked teams in the nation. The game is played in the Rose Bowl Stadium in Pasadena, California, and usually takes place on New Year's Day. As a regular participant in the game, the Big Ten is closely associated with the Rose Bowl. Michigan took part in the first Rose Bowl game in 1902, defeating Stanford 49–0. (It was also the first postseason college football game ever played.) In 1946, the Big Ten signed an exclusive agreement with the Rose Bowl, arranging an annual postseason matchup between teams from the Big Ten and

The Future of College Football's Postseason

There is currently heavy debate among schools and coaches as to whether college football should implement a playoff system to determine its national champion. Until 1998, the national champion was determined by polls in which members of the media voted to rank the best teams in the country. This system led to much controversy, as voting was highly subjective and teams did not control their own destiny. Teams could (and did) go undefeated and still not win the championship.

The present arrangement, known as the Bowl Championship Series (BCS), is an attempt to determine the national champion on the field by matching the two top-rated teams in a championship game. This setup has not ended the controversy, however, as the teams' rankings are determined by a computer calculation that many people find flawed.

Advocates for a football playoff system point to the highly successful NCAA basketball tournament, where the national champion is determined in a sixty-four-team tournament. Many football coaches agree that a playoff system of some nature would be ideal, but there are many obstacles to implementing a tournament. Some people argue that a playoff system, since it would last for a period of time, would hurt players academically by keeping them out of the classroom. Others are reluctant to end the current bowl arrangement because the games are highly profitable for both the schools and the conferences.

A full stadium watches as the Michigan Wolverines take on the University of Southern California Trojans at the 2007 Rose Bowl in Pasadena, California.

the Pac-10. The game's popularity soared, and the Rose Bowl has sold out every year since 1947.

Michigan has posted an 8–12 record in twenty trips to the Rose Bowl, the most appearances of any Big Ten school. In fact, only the University of Southern California (USC) has more appearances, with thirty-one. The two teams have faced each other eight times in the Rose Bowl; USC is ahead with a 6–2 record. Ohio State has the second-most appearances of any Big Ten team, earning the trip on thirteen occasions and compiling a record of 6–7.

GLOSSARY

All-America A national honor given every season to the conferences' top player at each position.

Bowl Championship Series (BCS) Five bowl games pairing the top ten teams in the nation against each other, highlighted by the national championship game in which the two top-ranked teams play.

bowl game A postseason college football game featuring two teams with winning records.

Bronko Nagurski Trophy Award given each year to college football's best defensive player; named after former Minnesota defensive tackle and fullback Bronko Nagurski.

Butkus Award Trophy given each year to the nation's top linebacker; named after former Illinois linebacker Dick Butkus.

center snap The practice of starting each play with the middle offensive lineman handing or tossing the ball to the quarterback.

defensive back Position whose primary responsibility is to guard an opposing team's wide receivers and defend against the pass.

flea-flicker A trick play developed by Illinois coach Bob Zuppke in which the running back accepts the handoff from the quarterback, only to laterally pass the ball back to the quarterback, who then attempts a forward pass.

gridiron Slang term for a football field.

handoff Play in which the quarterback hands the ball to the running back.

Heisman Trophy Award voted on by members of the media and given every year to college football's best player, regardless of position.

huddle Between plays, the practice of each team meeting in a circle behind the line of scrimmage to discuss the next play.

innovative Characterized by or introducing an original idea, method, or device; taking a new or different approach.

lateral pass Tossing or passing the ball sideways or backward.

Lombardi Award Trophy awarded annually to the nation's best collegiate offensive or defensive lineman; named after Vince Lombardi, the legendary football coach.

longevity The length or duration of an activity.

mentor A teacher or leader from whom one learns.

National Collegiate Athletic Association (NCAA) The organization that oversees college athletics.

onside kick A short kick that is intended to travel the minimum distance (10 yards) before the kicking team can legally attempt to recover the ball.

perennial Continually or consistently taking place.

pigskin Slang term for a football.

practice dummy A piece of equipment that is used by players to practice blocking; invented by Chicago coach Amos Alonzo Stagg.

prestigious Having a high honor or position.

prominence Standing out as being successful or well known.

protégé A student; someone who learns from a teacher or mentor.

reverse A trick play in which a ball carrier starts running in one direction but then hands the ball to another player, who is running in the opposite direction.

rivalry A very competitive relationship between people or teams.

Rose Bowl The oldest bowl game in the country, played every year in Pasadena, California. It features the Big Ten and Pac-10 conference champions.

screen pass A short pass to a running back who is protected by blockers.

FOR MORE INFORMATION

Big Ten Conference
1500 West Higgins Road
Park Ridge, IL 60068-6300
(847) 696-1010
Web site: http://bigten.cstv.com

National Collegiate Athletic Association (NCAA)
700 W. Washington Street
P.O. Box 6222
Indianapolis, IN 46206-6222
(317) 917-6222
Web site: http://www.ncaa.org

National Football Foundation's College Football Hall of Fame
111 South St. Joseph Street
South Bend, IN 46601
(800) 440-FAME (3263)
(574) 235-9999
Web site: http://www.collegefootball.org

Web Sites

Due to the changing nature of Internet links, Rosen Publishing has developed an online list of Web sites related to the subject of this book. This site is updated regularly. Please use this link to access the list:

http://www.rosenlinks.com/icfo/fb10

FOR FURTHER READING

Bradley, Michael. *Big Games: College Football's Greatest Rivalries*. Dulles, VA: Potomac Books, 2006.

DeCock, Luke. *Great Teams in College Football History*. Chicago, IL: Raintree Publishing, 2006.

Knapp, Ron. *Top 10 College Football Coaches*. Berkeley Heights, NJ: Enslow Publishers, 1999.

Ours, Robert M. *Bowl Games: College Football's Greatest Tradition*. Yardley, PA: Westholme Publishing, 2004.

Pellowski, Michael J. *The Little Giant Book of Football Facts*. New York, NY: Sterling Publishing, 2005.

Savage, Jeff. *Top 10 Heisman Trophy Winners*. Berkeley Heights, NJ: Enslow Publishers, 1999.

BIBLIOGRAPHY

Bentley Historical Library. "Michigan vs. Ohio State: 'Big Game' Decides Big Ten Title." 2002. "Michigan vs. Ohio State: Woody vs. Bo." 2002. "University of Michigan Football Coaches: Glenn E. (Bo) Schembechler." Retrieved December 26, 2006 (http://bentley.umich.edu).

Big Ten Conference. *Official Big Ten Centennial Football Guide*. Chicago, IL: Triumph Books, 1995.

Big Ten Conference. "2006 Season in Review." 2007. Retrieved January 12, 2007 (http://bigten.cstv.com/sports/m-footbl/spec-rel/011207aaa.html).

Gophersports.com. "Paul Bunyan's Axe—Minnesota vs. Wisconsin." 2007. "The Little Brown Jug—Minnesota vs. Michigan." Retrieved January 5, 2007 (http://www.gophersports.com).

Hyman, Mervin D., and Gordon S. White Jr. *Big Ten Football: Its Life and Times, Great Coaches, Players, and Games*. New York, NY: Macmillan Publishing Co., 1977.

Kazalia, John. About.com. "Michigan vs. Ohio." Retrieved January 2, 2007 (http://columbusoh.about.com/cs/historygenealogy/a/ohiomichigan_2.htm).

Mullin, John. *Tales from the Chicago Bears Sidelines*. Champaign, IL: Sports Publishing, 2003.

National Football Foundation's College Football Hall of Fame. "Hall of Famers." Retrieved December 17, 2006 (http://www.collegefootball.org/halloffamers.php).

Purdue Intercollegiate Athletics. "Joe Tiller Profile." "Traditions: Trophy Rivalries." Retrieved January 2007 (http://purduesports.cstv.com).

Richards, Gregory B., and Melissa H. Larson. *Big-10 Football*. New York, NY: Crescent Books, 1987.

University of Chicago. "Amos Alonzo Stagg." Retrieved December 26, 2006 (http://athletics.uchicago.edu/history/history-stagg.htm).

University of Michigan Athletics. "Lloyd Carr: Head Coach." Retrieved December 27, 2006 (http://mgoblue.com/coach_bio.cfm?bio_id=299&section_id=257&top=2&level=3).

INDEX

About the Author

Gabriel Kaufman was raised in Urbana, Illinois, in the heart of Big Ten country. A life-long Big Ten football fan, he graduated from the University of Illinois, where he spent many weekends watching games at Memorial Stadium. Kaufman works in educational publishing and has written four books for children. He currently lives in Brooklyn, New York.

Photo Credits

Cover top, bottom, pp. 6 right, 14 right 15, 19, 22, 23 right, 30 left, 33 right 36, 41 © Getty Images; pp. 4–5, 38 University of Wisconsin; pp. 6 left, 14 left , 23 left , 33 left © www.istockphotos. com/Stefan Klein; p. 7 © Oscar White/Corbis; p. 8 Purdue University Special Collections; pp. 11, 28 © AP Images; p. 17 Collegiate Images; p. 20 Purdue University; p. 24 Courtesy Gerald R. Ford Library; p. 25 College Football Hall of Fame; p. 30 right, 36 University of Michigan; p. 34 Ohio State University Archives.

Designer: Tom Forget
Photo Researcher: Marty Levick